Poems by
Jim Hughes
Rowena M Love
Michael Malone
Sheila Templeton

# *running threads*

MAKAR PRESS

First published in February 2006
by Makar Press, Troon

www.makarpress.co.uk

British Library Cataloguing in Publication Data
A catalogue record for this book is available
from the British Library.

ISBN 0-9547084-4-X
ISBN 978-0-9547084-4-X

Designed by Douglas Merritt ARCA

Printed by The Jane Street Printing Company
Edinburgh

# Contents

# Contents

# Contents

# Foreword

Richard Holloway,
*Chairman,*
*Scottish Arts Council*

In the last year the Makar Poets have evolved from a publishing collective into a highly entertaining, successful poetry performance group with a unique style.

They have made their excellent work accessible to hosts of folk for whom poetry is a new experience, as well as delighting established enthusiasts, and drawing praise from the professional literary community.

Weaving themes together like the running threads of the title, their work offers us a rich cloth of the poets' individual colours, which like their public performances, interweaves their own poetry with the living responses of their audiences.

This collection is a real testament to how the four poets have evolved in their enriching collaboration.

# Communion

*Sheila Templeton*

I'll buy you an apple,
so I can watch you cut it.

Slowly peeling skin back
from each segment; translucent
petals arranged like green lipped
lilies on your plate. Sliding a wafer
on to your tongue, letting it
dissolve in grainy sweetness.

We don't need two apples,
even if you know how I eat
mine, bursting the tight skin
with my teeth, winey apple spit
and flavour exploding as one.

You watch me take my bite,
then I'll watch you.

# Sunday Morning

*Michael Malone*

The way you spoon
into the bow of my back
and your hand reaches
over and down.

The way 'yes' floats out
high on a giggle when I
turn to ease your reach.

The way heat meets
in that space between us
and my flesh swells
to fill your grip.

The way we linger against
each other, joined at the groin,
the heart and the eyes.

The way you then sing,
'Morning'.

# Sitting with Maisie

*Sheila Templeton*

Her head fits exactly into the cup
of her mother's hand. Delicate fingers
curling around like fine pale wool.
Yet a whole person already
in her sleeping face.

Mouth opening and closing
like the little fish she's been.
Until now.
Swaddled against
this new element of air.

And we too are folded
in a beautiful silence
of looking at new life.
Looking at the whole world
in this baby girl.

It's the gloaming
and Maisie is one day old.

*Sunday June 6th 2004*

# Angry prayer

*Jim Hughes*

You pick me up,
face streaked with furious tears,
and wrap me in your blanket.

Against my face, it is rough
with unanswered questions,
yet warm with enigmatic hope.

# A Welcome Touch

*Michael Malone*

Expression echoing the Majorcan sun,
he speaks to everyone,
fingers like spider limbs, resting

on shoulders, touching cheeks
that politely remain available
for his silken touch.

Uncaring of the space
that rings us all, children
attract his special regard.

For them his smile
is long to enough to curve
under two pairs of eyes.

His eyes light upon
my two year old son, arachnoid hands
web under his small white face.

Tabloid thoughts push me to my feet
but they are dusted down by the brush
of Sam's soprano, 'Man. Nice man.'

Guiltily, I attempt to change my charge
into a greeting, and I am rewarded
by the heat of a wrinkled smile. Then I realise

age may have waxed white his hair,
bleached tone from his skin,
but has been unable to grey his youth.

# Daddy's Girl

*Sheila Templeton*

You were Alan Ladd. All chiselled
cheekbones and blond hair falling
into your eyes. I had no idea
you towered above him.
You towered over everybody.

At tea time I raced to meet you
my legs carefully bowed.
'Born in the saddle' you'd say
each day, sounding amazed.

We'd saddle up and gallop
through our canyon, chasing
maverick steers around the kitchen
until the ding of a chow wagon triangle
brought us sweaty to the table,
pushing stetsons back, hitching
horses to the old oak dresser.

'Pork an' beans AGAIN'
you'd say, looking down
at brimming plates of broth.
'No, pardner. Tonight,
it's Beans and Pork!'
Slapping our knees in glee
knowing who we were.

Until the night of my first
school Christmas party
where in my new blue silk
dress and butterfly hair slides
suddenly you couldn't see me.

But I always knew you.
You were Alan Ladd.

# A Daughter's Diary

*Michael Malone*

## Monday

The phone's siren heckled my thoughts,
an electric shock wedging me into the present.
It was Mother. Said she was coming. Said
she would be fit to visit after all. At the weekend.
Six days stretch before me, coloured red
like carpet, minus the cushioning.
Bickered with husband. Then the twins.
Suddenly they were too loud, too clumsy,
too... *there*. Nerves wound tighter
than wicker on a chair. Time to soak,
ease the flare of pain where neck meets shoulder.
From there it will travel at the speed of noise,
through muscle, skirt bone, slide down my forearm
moulder between second and third knuckle
in a rhythm to match piercing of the phone.

## Tuesday

'Sweet dreams?' Tim's face close, stagnant breath
easier to ignore than hard flesh pressed against my thigh.
'Thanks for the alarm cock.' I stumble to the toilet,
drunk on fatigue. Shouted in your sleep, he said.
Couldn't make it out, he said. But it was loud, he laughed.
Pain at nest in my skull.
House vacant today as usual.
No company but thought. Thought harasses and chases.
Thought slips in, slides in, shoots in. Thought clothed
in silent screams and teeth.
Housework won't do itself.
Work, work, busy, busy, work, work. Breathing
like a heat-soaked puppy. Forced calm, fists tight.
It's only mother, for fuck's sake!
Boys ape sharks' feeding frenzy at suppertime.
Tim's eyes at bedtime. Guilt gagged my reply. I lie
like cooling meat on a marble slab, while Tim
is chased by sweet, hot release, into his dreams.

## Wednesday

Tucked away a pill this morning. Seratonin
inserts the right tone in my life. Ribs coated
with the ghost of Pain Barely Remembered. Sleep
a near neighbour last night, each introduction
broken as memories leaked to the surface
like a gloop of oil from the bed of a brackish pond.
Tim read to the boys at bedtime.
Usual pattern of limbs under eiderdown.
They were all eyes, teeth... casual affection.
Me, cast as observer, peering over the garden fence.
'What's wrong, Love?' Tim's arm harder to shoulder
than his groin. Tried to deflect his thoughts there.
With a squeeze.
'Don't you just want a cuddle?' He moved out of reach.
'Are you gay?' I flee. Cradle my confusion on the couch.
A ceiling apart, for the first time. Arms shelter ribs.
The girl remembers her mother, eyes big,
hair everyday electric. Corded forearms,
fingers like bird claws. A mother's fear
she will drop her child.  Daughter only allowed
shallow breaths. A mother's fear,
she will be to blame for a daughter's brain
skinning the pavement with bone fragments,
matter and hair.  Temazapam
on the menu tonight, madam.
We have a pill for every occasion.

## Thursday

_____
_____
_____
_____
_____
_____

## Friday

Soften your gaze; look to one side of your future,
you will see in its outline the shape of your past.
On one side I see smoke hanging before a window
breath clears and a girl grips the hem
of her mother's trouser, stares while other children
jostle and jump. All cocoon and no play
allows Sue to have knees without blemish,
teeth without chips, but fractures
the green twig of her psyche. Went for a swim today.
Forgot what the kiss of water felt like full-length on the skin.
This was a daughter's almost daily defiance.
If the skin couldn't break Mother needn't know.
What she doesn't know is my jaw muscles
bunched like grapes today.
Anger ground against my teeth. Enough.
I've been in the glacial heat of childbirth.
Twice, for fuck's sake.

Better go. One of the boys has coated the pan
(and some of the floor) in a delightful tan with his supper.
Only Mummy's hand can ease the sand-rub of pain.
Illness makes his eyes bigger than Bambi's. So cute.
Better sleep with Tim tonight. Better groan as well;
sound as if I'm enjoying it.
Then we won't interrupt Mother's sleep
with banging bedsprings.
Doubt if she's been 'banged' since Daddy died.
Doubt she would know what it means.
Did mother look past the outline of her future
and bandage me against a past she didn't want to repeat?
Ooh, the smell. Outlines my nostrils. Better go.

## Saturday

Amazing, isn't it. A few well-placed groans.
Actually enjoyed it. Swam in the calm this morning.
Could still feel Tim, moisture amid caress of water.
Mum arrived at suppertime. Boys grabbed
the proffered toys and charged into the street.
Hands wedged into her purple cardigan, she watched them
slide along the path in their new skates.
'Thank you.' My voice hollow.
'You would never have bought me those,'
escaped before I could stop it.
'You were always a little scaredy-cat.'
Her reply hung in the air between us. Burst a bruising.
Something bubbled in my stomach, shone up my throat
and jumped from behind my lips. All eyes locked on me.
'What's so funny?' Mum and Tim echoed.
Another bubble leapt to join the first.
More teased open my jaw,
added heat to my cheeks. They were teeming for release.
Popping around my ears, paying no heed to Mum's
measured attempt to join in. She, a seal slapping flippers.
Healing tears bounced down my face, evaporated
into the mirth I weaved through the room
dressing the future against the weal of the past.

# A Touching Place

*Jim Hughes*

She has travelled all her life,
dragging leg irons of disease,
to reach here.

This very spot.

In her aching belly,
need has grown to desperation.
It drives her through her terror
and the gawking crowd.

He has travelled all his life
to reach here.

This very spot.

His shoulders ache with the weariness of others,
his brow lacerated by their twisted expectations.

Now her fingers tremble as they stretch
and brush the mud spattered hem of his robe.

She finds a touching place.

You and I
have travelled our separate ways to here.

This very spot.

We stumble and trip over
our failure and success.

Driven by our need and compassion
we stretch out tentative fingers
and find in each other

a touching place.

# Hot Tub

*Rowena M Love*

Ticktockticktockticktockticktock.
I feel the clock's cutting edge,
second hand slicing into me at every pass.
Haveyoudonethis? Haveyoudonethat?
Why not? Do it now. Now. Now. Now.
Demands ring in my ears,
echoing, rebounding. Loud.
Things done, not done, unable to be undone,
a crushing weight on my chest.

I slip outside to the hot tub,
a giant bucket of moonlight
shimmering in December night.
I ease myself into its amniotic fluid,
where I can enjoy the darkness, the warmth.
The peace.
Muscles uncoil at jets' behest,
while spray from their bubbles
coat my face like tears;
I smile in pleasure.
Stress evaporates,
unsubstantial as the steam swirling
in tonight's chill air.
Soak over, I rise like Venus;
reborn in relaxation.

## Burnout

*Jim Hughes*

He read an article about burnout.
About him.

No, he thought,
I'm still burning.
More slowly perhaps,
but getting there.

# Hot Chick

*Sheila Templeton*

Ma man sez
'Yer... HOT.'
Ah sez 'Mmm'
in his ear.
He sez 'Naw
yer HOT, ah mean
sizzlin,' hen, ah
could fry an egg
oan yer back.
Whit's wrang,
ur ye no weel ?
It's no verra comfy
fur me.
Yerr like a toasty
hot water bottle
a' the time.
Iz this whit thon
Germaine Greer
cries the Change?
Ur you huvven
a hot flush?'

'Naw,' ah sez,
'Ah'm huvven
a Power Surge.
An' you kin sleep
on the flerr.'

# Thoroughly Modern Man

*Michael Malone*

21st Century boy hide your penis.
Jam it back between your thighs,
press your unshaven chin against
your hollow chest, for you will be
nothing but a jester at court
whose audience follows the Queen
(for the King is long dead)
and laughs **at** you.

You will be 'up for the cup'
but find that it is filled with the piss
of they who hold society's conscience
cradled in weighted scales and judge
that two wrongs make a satisfying right.

'They' crowd statistics of abuse
onto our pages and screens certifying
that our pathetic pricks
make us worthless; statistics that jostle
with pixelated images of man crawling
towards a pair of stilettoed heels.

21st Century boy indict your father,
for he nailed his tongue to a mast
of indifference, while pushing his penis
so far back that it was inserted
fluidly into his own rectum.

# Love Underground

*Sheila Templeton*

They look like they've been here a long time.
On the underground for sixty years, sharing
a seat 'Appreciated by the Elderly and Infirm.'
Grown pale together, lengthened their limbs
like cranes. He carries her Liz Claiborne bag
tenderly. Puts up his hand to stroke
the sweet crease of her face.
Their heads move in harmony.
Nodding mandarin dolls. Stork legs entwine,
discreetly rubbing ankles. Hands shaking
in a rhythm of life long syncopation.
She leans towards him to whisper a secret
and their laughter fills the carriage
as it rattles along towards Hillhead.

# A Guiding Hand

*Michael Malone*

The back of his hand
primed with liver spots,
placed in the middle
of the small of her back,
his touch as light as a promise
wrapped in love and faith,
he guides her past the crush
of flushed shoppers, past their gaze
as impersonal as an embalmer's.

With each touch he celebrates
a lifetime of short days.
With each touch she tucks
an imaginary loose, grey hair
back in its place. With each touch
she flows as if fresh poured.

I look at my own wife with a flame
forgotten in the warmth of constancy
and guide her with a hand blushed
with youth past the unfocused stares
of strangers, through the crowds
of applauding pigeons and between
cars racing to the next junction.

She stops walking and faces me
her expression blank as an empty
page on a computer screen, save
for the cursor of irritation
flashing in her eyes and says,
'Will you stop pushing me?'

# Presents and Absence

*Rowena M Love*

Presents breed beneath an artificial tree;
size and quantity valued more than thought
or time.

No time left – for you're no longer here.
No instant fix of comfort and joy
for me this year –
just cold turkey
followed by mince pies and sighs.

While white berries glisten their tears
for the missed kisses of mistletoe,
the family's conscience pricks and jags
in an abundance of holly.
Their dutiful deeds smother me
with an ivy stranglehold.

I'm encircled by wreaths
dark as depression,
except for red-berried guilt
glowing like coals of Hell
among the glossy green leaves.

Conversation is carefully wrapped
in glib messages of goodwill:
tissue thin and easily torn,
only the Sellotape® of good intentions
holds it together.

I'm so cold.
Alone,
yet constantly surrounded;
a footprint in slowly melting snow.

# Christmas Child

*Jim Hughes*

Christmas child…
you stand at our stable door
bearing the unwrapped gift
of terrible, unrelenting love.

You will us to be born
again, and again, and again.

# Keekin In

*Rowena M Love*

Kye[1] coorie in thir sta,
life smokin fae thir mous[2];
a leam o sunlicht thirls[3] the mirk
lik guid news
an splatters braiths wi gowd[4].

Anent[5] the wa, a cuddy,
wi its timmer fraucht[6]:
siller board set wi cairngorms
that myrrh the air.

Nae bairnie nor hirds[7] are here,
nor kings wi camels;
only angels the sleepin doos[8],
yet the morn's[9] rich
wi frankinscence
o promise.

[1] *kye* = cows; *coorie* = snuggle, nestle
[2] *mous* = mouths
[3] *thirls the mirk* = pierces the gloom
[4] *gowd* = gold
[5] *anent the wa* = beside the wall;
*cuddy* = a donkey; joiner's trestle
[6] *timmer fraucht* = timber burden
[7] *hirds* = shepherds
[8] *doos* = doves
[9] *the morn* = morning; tomorrow.

# Father Martin

*Michael Malone*

Years have cast a haze
over the man who gave me the chess set.
The line of his nose may have been broken
by spectacles, his hair
may have been seasoned grey.

I was so short. He seemed a giant.
He was a giant, but was he tall?
He taught me how to play,
where to find whelks,
how not to abuse privilege.
All of those lonely convent children
and he gave the chess set to me.

I found it in a cupboard
unopened after three house moves
and twenty-five years.
One piece missing,
its foam outline empty
as the space behind a mirror.

The set is dusted with memory of his voice,
'Guilt and religion should be strangers.'
'We mourn ourselves, not our dead.'
'Going to Mass weekly is not the measure of the
man.'

I was nine.
I understood every word.

# Silence

Jim Hughes

And now silence.

It seeps into the creaking hinges
of my heart.

The only sound, the in-breath of God,
before he whispers.

# Requiem for a Son

*Sheila Templeton*

These impossible arches, graceful bridges
to take us to your heaven.
Wood smoothed by five hundred years
to silk under my hand.
All made by man to shout out your glory.

I will not weep here.

Once I carried him, laughing, high on my shoulders.
Now I wait for his comrades to carry him
under a brave flag,
to set him down at your altar, where bright light
spills like blood from the window.
Your great sacrifice for mankind.

I am not able to weep in this place.

They sent me back his cap badge,
a sturdy silvered stag.
Made to last for years. And so was he.
Bydand says the badge. Courage.
A word with too much space.
Sometimes truth hides in the spaces between words.
I see no truth here.

And I cannot weep.

It's not here I shall remember him.
I need to stand alone under the cold spinning of stars.
The empty sky respects my tears.

At least it will be cold there, like his grave.
And I can hold on to sharp salt crusted grass
until my palms are scored and bleeding.

## For Annie

*Rowena M Love*

Like thyme clinging to a wall,
you stayed in her heart,
just as she does mine.
No earth for roots, yet you held tight
scenting her every day with thoughts of you:
memories of a time before the war,
dreams of what would not be.

So I had my hadj laid out:
as she lies alone in a spinster's grave,
I'd visit you on her behalf,
hand-delivering a flower
that was nearly eighty years in the growing.

Train trip dreich as her life without you
showed soggy glimpses of French countryside:
an age-worn tapestry knotted with cemeteries
where silver warp of stones glitter
through grassy weft.
At Arras I took a taxi, cold and damp.
Wipers ticked their metronome,
counting time for a song no longer sung.
Side-trip to an unknown florist,
marble mausoleum crammed with blooms,
their colours November-dimmed.
Then the rain beating on your gravestone,
as it must do hers,
crooning the same dirge for you both.

I took out one rose, put it safe
to carry home to where she lies
in her lair above the Clyde.

# H.M. Iolaire (Shipwrecked 1919)

*Michael Malone*

The great guns were silent
yet boomed still in the ears
of ragged Lewis men journeying home
on the eve of hope. Soldiers
returning from a mud-slimed land
crowded the ship's deck, eager to see again
wives, mothers and others whose features
had been dulled by a sea of fog and gas.

Trench tight on the Iolaire
they prayed a hungry wind
would cleanse mud and blood
frozen in a death mask of memory.

But the same wind scenting blood
whipped, chased and drove waves
with mounting fury, knowing the greed
of the Beasts of Holm for the flesh
of man. A hunger not satisfied
since the sea was freed from ice.

There, with the lights of Stornoway
hovering in welcome,
Iolaire was razed on the rocks
by the giant claw of cruel irony,
sailor's lungs were swollen with salted despair.
Another 200 souls lost and ground
on fate's granite snout.

# Summertime

*Sheila Templeton*

Summertime was the unmarried aunts
hurrying in from the ice cream van,
their booty of vanilla piled high
in an old baking bowl,
like a wedding celebration
melting in laughter.

Straightening stocking seams,
they shouted for lemonade, better still
a big bottle of American Cream Soda,
long spoons and the tallest glasses
from the kitchen press.

We sat outside, legs dangling
from a scarred bench made of old
railway sleepers, stirring our floats

pearling clear glass with sticky strands
set forever in beaded DNA of memory.

# Makin Pancakes

*Rowena M Love*

Tastin the pancake, mindins o ma great-aunt
seem thick as butter Ah'd spreid therr:
efternuins wi the douce dame that sugared ma ginger
fur fear Ah'd git gas.
It wud volcano up and o'er the gless,
its leemonade lava poorin doon the sides
afore finin its ain level oan the marble coonter.
Sweet bit flat, Ah guzzlet it doon, gritty syrup an a,
whaur Ah sat tucked high oan hur bentwood chair,
legs hingin.

Then oan tae the best joab: makin drap scones,
aye the same teacup wi its fadin rose yaised as measure,
same spuin[1] skiddlin the batter in the muckle broun bowl.
Staunin oan the chair noo, peenie[2] girdet roon ma middle,
twice roon fur it tae fit,
wi Auntie's airms the kinch[3] tae keep it oan.
Ah hud tae beat the batter hard
til it soundet lik weans plowterin[4] in the burn,
then, drap bi drap oan the het girdle,
Ah makkit letters for a in the hoose
afore feenishin wi ordinar roons.
Watchin fur the bubbles as sign
fur me tae turn them, usin hur blade
whase bane haunle[5] had lang syne departet
afore tuckin them up warm in a tea towel,
cosy in thir linen as me wi hur.

[1] *spuin* = spoon
[2] *peenie* = apron; *girdet* = tied
[3] *kinch* = knot
[4] *plowterin* = splashing; *burn* = stream
[5] *bane haunle* = bone handle; *lang syne* = long since

# Old Hat

*Jim Hughes*

Mistress Mildred Macumbie's hat sits
firmly on her head.

It hasn't much option
pinioned fast, as it is,
to an improbable breaking surf
of blue rinsed waves.
Lacquered hard.

Despite this, with a freedom enjoyed
only by better class millinery,
it scans the length and breadth
of Glasgow's newest Starbucks.

At the next table,
four Kelvinside matrons, carefully
maintained and in good running order,
scrutinise diaries
and each other's crow's feet.

A couple, in the far corner,
avoid each other's eyes,
and exchange assorted silences.
The married kind.

The hat sighs nostalgically, and compares
the scene, unfavourably,
with Miss Cranston's Tearoom,
half a century gone,
where etiquette would have ensured
polite conjugal congress.
Conversation only, you will understand.

# Little Sleeve

*Sheila Templeton*

These are not my arms,
these lardy bits, bulging.

They grew in the night.
Along with trailing wings
like a lizard's webbed oxter.

Maybe if I paint
my nails
HOT
SCARLET?

Sit all evening,
elbows bent,
firming the droops.

'Madam, a little sleeve is
so nice... on the older lady.'

Fuck your little sleeve.
There's my frock.
There.
That one.
The rhinestone satin...
with the shoe string straps.

# Breast Screening

*Sheila Templeton*

They nearly had to strap me down.

'Fuller bosomed ladies find
it's no so bad,' said the nurse.

Aye. Right.

She picks up my right breast
in one hand, weighing, slapping it
across a cold metal shelf, smoothing,
flattening, like a lump of dough.

Slap slap pat pat slap again
into stretched out new plucked
chicken fillet, blue veined,
lilac tinted, ready for breadcrumbs.

Down comes a cider press
contraption to make sure
this one behaves, has no thought
of springing back to boobness.

'Stay there please. We'll need
another shot.'
I look at my two dimensional
right bosom, flat as a plate,
and wonder how we'll ever manage
to get joined up again.
Will she bring a different machine
to restore 2 D to 38 D?

'That's you then, no so bad
was it ? Results will be posted
in three to four weeks.'

Aye. Right.

# Lucozade, Grapes and Silence

*Michael Malone*         *For Jonathan Watson*

They come bearing gifts,
tread past the other beds,
a forced expression flat on their faces
that says life is normal,
my friend isn't a cancer colander.
They hand over the drink and fruit
and hide behind the donation
while they echo inanities,
dressed up with smiles as hesitant
as a child on a stranger's doorstep.

The air is fogged with silence.
While they tick off in their minds
what not to say, I prepare
to give them a reminder of me.
But what do you say when all you've seen
are the veins that trace the inside of your eyelids?
All you've touched is crisp, white cotton
and pain?

I hoist a smile that, if it were a flag
would sail at the top of the mast
and will words to a tongue that feels
as lifeless as a strip of leather. They laugh.
The heat from this sound
raises the bounty of more energy
and I tell them the one about the cancer patient
and the bottle of Lucozade.

# The Dolphin

*Rowena M Love*          *for Insa*

Cancer's a queer fish:
anaemic amoeba endlessly mutating;
puffer-fish growths bloated with poison;
or shoals of cells
that prowl like piranhas
stripping my health in their feeding frenzy.

But attitude can attack back,
till I'm the dolphin swimming free
from this sea
of sickness.

I'll trawl my system,
catching cancers and fears,
netting them to wriggle and squirm:
powerless.

I'm the dolphin swimming free.

Modern medicine may have me filleted,
canned and processed,
pumped full of additives –
but the rest is up to me...

I'm the dolphin swimming free.

Dread might dorsal my spine,
tears flood my face with brine
but I... CAN... DO... THIS...

I am the dolphin swimming free.

## Like a Sneeze

*Michael Malone*

She did say she loved me
after each of the births.
'I' came out slow and unsure
of itself from behind fused teeth.
'Love you' burst out like a sneeze.
Then she studied the wise
new face of the child
as if searching for the mockery
she was certain was there.

And she did give me a hug.
One, when the dog died.
And one at Christmas
the year our son drew me his first
card. It was nice, all the same,
but it would have been nicer
if the air hadn't been squeezed
out of my lungs so fast.
Just like a sneeze.

And then, at the end
when I said 'I love you'
enough for the both of us,
like it would stop
the march of her illness,
like it would stop her pallor
from yellowing further,
I wanted to touch her nose
my fingers dusted with pepper,
just enough to allow
one more sneeze.

# Scream

*Jim Hughes*

*Dance, called the waves*
*but I would not dance.*

*Sing, called the wind*
*but I would not sing*

You bitch!
I choke with rage as I scream at you
across the years,
a scream you stifled as I lay alone, terrified,
in that darkened creaking ward.

I longed for soft warm arms,
but you bound me in ice hard sheets,
and strangled me with your eyes.

You threatened greater terror
under searing theatre lights,
frightened flesh,
breaking steel.

From bricks of despair
I built my wall.

I ache for these lost years,
for sleep unslept,
for tears unwept.

*Weep, sighed my soul*
*and I wept*
*and I danced*
*and I sang.*

## For Worse

*Michael Malone*

*for Doris*

Coloured grey,
gilded with sweat,
large enough to grind
flour for the world's poor;
granite hangs around her neck.

Every movement
a study in effort,
every thought seeps into stone.

She can never leave his side.

He cries for attention.
She sees the man
and forgets the child.

She waits the thrill of the phone;
someone else's life.
She dreams of better times,
resents the vow that doesn't list
what 'for worse' might entail.

But if she can forget the wife
and be the woman
for a rosary of moments,
it may save them both.

# The Carousel

*Rowena M Love*

Neither admitted the other could be right,
which fuelled their fury, cranked worry's wheel,
so the carousel turned in their endless fight.

Taking no prisoners soon deepened their plight:
transforming decisions to the hardest steel –
neither admitted the other could be right.

Damsel disappointed in her so-called knight,
frequented unfair ground that wasn't quite real:
so the carousel turned in their endless fight.

Spicing each meal with gratuitous spite,
they salted their wounds until they'd never heal:
neither admitted the other could be right.

Vitriol bubbled at the argument's height,
searing and scarring with horrendous zeal;
so the carousel turned in their endless fight.

How could they admit they'd completely lost sight
of whatever it was that they used to feel?
Neither admitted the other could be right,
so the carousel turned in their endless fight.

## Scars

*Sheila Templeton*

Old scars need time to soften from their frostbite,
thinned lips still stiffened by years of lonely cold.
But time had not joined us in the bed that night.

We tried the language of fingertips to write
the missing words of love, what could not be told.
Old scars need time to soften from their frostbite.

Appendix? I thought so. The place is right.
Raw story space, fingers aching to unfold.
But time had not joined us in the bed that night.

And you've had a C-section. Cut vertical, straight.
Nowadays they're kinder. Hidden, not bold.
Old scars need time to soften from such frostbite.

The truth is, scars are best looked at by candlelight.
Nuzzled, nibbled, licked to melt-down gold.
But time had not joined us in the bed that night.

So much not said, yet waiting, in roughened white.
Aching to be used, to break fear's stranglehold.
Old scars need time to soften from their frostbite,
but time had not joined us in the bed that night.

# Osiris

*Jim Hughes*

Oil rig Osiris views his dead creation,
the stillness of sterility.

It is acid green.
Gangrenous scar tissue
of a wound too dead to fester,

Numb plastic condemned
to life within itself.
No friendly rust to help it on its way.
No restless grub to eat it back to life.

He allows no resurrecting death,
nor opening of tomb.

## Veni, Vidi, Vici

*Michael Malone*

They came
to the waters of Holy Loch, Dunoon
pointed Polaris at the threat from the cold east
and prepared for their self-appointed part
as the world's policeman.

They saw hills haloed in cloud,
clothed in verdant vestments of trees,
grass and heather genuflecting before an altar
of water sanctified with lush life.

They congested the once deep loch
defiled it with three decades of insult,
paid for our hospitality with 20,000 tonnes
of rusted cancerous pieces of silver.

They left us with a thinning broom
in search of another cause.
Another war.
Another Eden.

# Genocide

*Jim Hughes*

Genocide is easy,
Genos don't bleed.

Genocide is easy,
others take the lead.

Genocide is easy,
they all look much the same.

Genocide is easy,
the telly numbs the pain.

Genocide is easy,
it happens way out there.

Genocide is easy,
of course we really care.

Genocide is easy,
it isn't me or you.

Genocide is easy,
what else can we do?

Genocide is...hold it there,
you ca................

# The Clearances

*Michael Malone*

In the days that were to number her last,
shivering under plaid threadbare as hope,
she had snow-laden skies for a roof,
chill rock and earth to heat her back.

Three days since they arrived with a writ
but still the smoke rolled thick and black.
Still, she could hear the whine of dogs,
the bark of orders and the cries for justice
from men, women and children.

Evicted from this green fold of earth
where cattle and crop won the battle
to feed her and her clan, they were driven
to a stretch of rock by the sea
where soil was too thin to embrace seed
and where wind came without pause
from the Arctic wastes.

Generations fought and thrived here
but now the glen was empty save for
the dark smoke of the burnings. 'Where
was her clan?' She appealed to the sky.
Folded tight in the hold of a ship
typhus bound for the New World?
Fumbling with fish knives on the stark coast?
Or lost, in a Glasgow slum?

She wasn't aware that her Laird
his dirk blunted by greed
had cut the ties that held him to his people;
that his sons had forsworn the Gaelic
as barbaric. She only knew that the bustle
of her family had already been replaced
by the placid bleating of a million sheep.

# Song of Wallace

*Rowena M Love*    *'I have brought you to the ring, now see if you can dance[1]'*

In the discord of distant days,
seven hundred years ago,
came this hero
on a legendary scale,
his huge sword a baton
conducting men in pitched battle
until betrayal's false note spoiled the tune.
To the enemy's chorus of jeers,
the Guardian faced his grisly death
with the same pride and courage
he'd led his life –
and ours.

Dead but not silenced,
for Wallace was more than a passing note
in the libretto of liberty
sung by so many Scots –
his was the very melody at its core;
a leitmotiv of patriotism
guaranteed,
even now,
to stir the blood
at the merest echo of his name
and have our hearts dancing.

[1] Wallace's words to his army before the battle of Falkirk

# A Bonnie Fechter

*Sheila Templeton*

That winter, snaw flew its feathers thick
smoorichin the hale Rannoch Moor.
I thocht the warld wud be white for iver.
Danny the Keeper said the stags
wud have tae come doon,
else they'd sterve tae death.

We'd niver seen red deer afore.
But these beasts wernae ony shade o red.
Ivery day as the licht hid ahint the Black Mounth,
they floated ower the high fence
at the side o the line,
sepia angels biggen a brig ower cloudy drifts
against a grape slate sky. I thocht their hooves
could niver touch the grun,

until the day we heard a scraping
ootside the kitchen door. He was big.
His antlers telt a lang story, a hero's story,
of territory defended and hinds protected.
He eased back a bittie, but didnae flee.
At my mither's nod, I threw the tattie peelings
scudding intae the kirned up khaki snaw.

And waited and watched while he took his time,
his fine big heid lowered wi nae loss o dignity.
And so he lat me feed him ivery day,
as the licht left the sky.
Nae to touch or stroke, but he'd lat me
look intae his een and watch him,

until the day he didnae come. The day I looked
and shouted and poked aboot the frosty dyke.
But nae use. My pail o slippy tattie parings frozen
in the night where I'd left it.
I splashed bilin water tae saften it for him.
But nae sign.

Winter gnawed on,

until Danny the Keeper said ower a nip and a fag
'Thon's a grand auld beast
deid doon by the burn.
Funny that. How they hide awa,
when they ken it's their time.
Like an auld war hero.
Like ony bonnie fechter
fan he kens his time is up.'

# Lost Villages o Doon

*Rowena M Love*

At Corbie Craigs[1]
hoose nor hut are staunin still,
the space whaur they were
teem[2],
brick an beam as broken
as the mines that fed them.
Benwhat near at haun,
higher up Lethanhill, Burnfoothill,
or Craigmark ablow
are jist as empty.
Beoch, tae, is a lang five mile
frae Da'mellin't'n tae history.

Wreaths are laid
fur the hames that were razed
as if ilka hoose itsel had deed.
Bit bide a wee
in the space whaur they were
and the echoes come real
shapes and sounds mair solid an sure
nor all yer trees an birdsang.

[1] Corbie Craigs, Benwhat, Lethanhill, Burnfoothill and
Craigmark were all villages near Dallmellington in the
Doon Valley area of Ayrshire.
[2] *teem* = empty, echoing, unoccupied

Mither at the mangle, her hauns red raw,
first o her sheets aready snappin wi a guid blaw;
faither scartin[3] last o the coal dust fae his face
wi his well-stropped cut-throat;
a footie gemm, lads efter scuil wi jerseys fur goals
or a sairious team, wi village pride their prod
tae gie their all;
weans plowterin[4] in the burn, squealin or greetin,
wee Jeannie's ribbon aye at the droop;
windaes flickerin bright wi lowes[5],
the fires' reek[6] as saft an grey as stags' velvet.

The villages arnae lost,
fur memories o they days
are mortared strang intae that hillside
far above the Doon.

---

3 *scartin* = scraping
4 *plowterin* = splashing
5 *lowes* = flames, fires
6 *reek* = smoke

# Going Home

*Sheila Templeton*

Peesie weeps and whaups shrieking
wheeling high above ploughed parks.
Granda's calloused hand holds mine.
We are watching oyster catchers
mincing in the shining shallow
waters of the quartz pebbled Don.

He wears faded flapping dungarees
with a craftsman's special pocket.
His bonnet covers bumpy bits
and narrow strands of hair. I lean
against his smell, freshly dusted
sawdust mixed through
Capstan Navy Full Strength.

We wonder at a salmon glistening
on a bed of fragrant weed.
Then like a serving spoon
the river flips it over.
We see what's underneath.

'Ach. Otters are right bonny beasts
but they're selfish wee buggers'

He shows me distant Bennachie
with Mither Tap glassing
black against its clouds. I listen
rapt to tales of vanished tribes
who built tall fires there, who
knew how to melt rock
and weld stones forever.

Then going home planting
my feet in Granda's prints,
in that careful space
down the side of a park
filled with young green corn.

# Playground

*Jim Hughes*

Above the school, a smudge of starlings
bank and swoop, practicing curved paint strokes
against grey November sky.

Then, as one, they straighten up
for that long haul South
to remembered sun.

In the playground, arms outstretched,
we jet-roar and twist
stuttering machine guns
in each other's faces.

Then, one by one,
we peel away
and start that long trek North
with only the faintest memory
of wings and sun on our lonely backs.

# Feeding the Birds

*Rowena M Love*

The dressing up box has been raided:
a smudged-lipstick robin primps on the fence;
chaffinches parade in fancy costumes;
a single crow clatters along roof tiles
in Mummy's high heels.

Sparrows play hide and seek through the bushes
or dart out for a game of tag;
blackbirds prefer Grandmother's Footsteps,
running and waiting, running and waiting,
scattered bread their goal.

Tits skip with clothesline,
waiting for their go on the swinging feeder,
while other birds bicker
over strewn-marble nuts.

School is out –
until unexpected movement
clears the playground.

# Heron

*Jim Hughes*

In the shallows, you stand
exquisitely balanced
on your dark reflection.

The power of great wings
mirrored in the strength
of your stillness.

# A Proverb Moon

*Rowena M Love*

An ancient mirror hangs in the sky,
its surface speckled with shadows
where silvering has flaked loose
to cluster in stars.
Clouds steam up its face,
blurring the image
till only a whisper of it
echoes in my eyes.
Then, as if fingers
had stroked through condensation,
cracks of light appear.

*Inspired by a Chinese proverb:*
*'The moon sinks like a mirror in the sky.'*

# In the Raw

*Michael Malone*

Naked toes probing
the deep pile bedroom carpet,
I stand braced in honesty
before the cruel length mirror.

Fine lines that crow
from the side of my eyes
not so difficult to find now.

Testosterone fused hairs bore
through pores on my nose and ears
I turn to appraise the rug
that is my neck, shoulders and back
while skin on my scalp reflects
each available beam of light
with laughing intensity.

Another grey hair sprouts
sternly from my chest
that doesn't quite need a bra
since I started to squeeze out
those press-ups. Mental note –
increase to five a day.

Shit! There's even one
dour hair on my belly.
I contain the relaxed flesh here
with outstretched fingers.
Enough blubber here to feed
a Polar Bear for a month.

The towel drops to snake
around my feet. There's still life
in the flesh hanging here
even if the opportunity for use
is as rare as cheer in a brothel.

To think the legs that prop me
used to pump around fields of cropped grass
rarely move below a canter
looked quite good in shorts
would not now look out of place
behind some chicken wire.

Eyes slowly rise to meet eyes
a man I think I know looks back.
Unanswered questions sulk
in the yolk of his eyes.

# Miss Sixty

*Sheila Templeton*

The morning I turned sixty, I stood in my kitchen
thinking about soup. Lentil, cullen skink, split pea
cock-a-leekie, vichysoisse, broth, even gazpacho,
which gave me a headache,

so I took to the beach,
all blowing and striding and sea-washed sky.
And ran as hard as I could, holding my arms out.
Pinned myself to the wind and flew, hanging
from my shoulders like a dress from a coat hanger,

looking down at council workmen,
busy with solemn spades and wheelbarrows,
shovelling up heaps of sand from the prom,
tipping it back on to the beach, where it lives,
but each winter, sneaks over, trying
to take over the town, creeping in,
like the sixty years of my life,
sidling up on me, piling up the decades.

I have not reached
the stage of trying to shovel
any years back, by tummy tucks,
face lifts or even just lying in my teeth.

But one thing I do know.
Soup doesn't have to be complicated.
In my kitchen, from today onwards,
I will make either Orangey-Red Soup.
Or Green Soup.

Leaving plenty of time for flying.

# The Causeway

*Rowena M Love*

Crossing the causeway to Grimsay,
the tide pushed a sunset to my feet.

Palette knife sandbars
crusted oily reds with gold:
Turner dabbling with drama
as colours ebbed and flowed.

On my other hand,
still water pooled,
pulling my eye
to a pale pastel water-colour
painted on glass:
moonrise.

Life's a causeway;
choices on either side.
Not necessarily good or bad –
just... different.

What counts,
more than what you choose,
is why.

# Taking New Heart

*Sheila Templeton*

I slung it into the first rock pool.
Left my heart to sink among sharp shells
and scuttling claws. More jelly fish
than pump. No more hope than a witch
trying to prove her innocence before God.

Waves fretted along the shore, offering
alternatives. A black heart, seductively
hard and shiny. But it was chipped.

Then its twin, in pulpy half-chewed
wood, too like my own for comfort.

A stone heart, buried in white sand,
Jacob's pillow. A child's swing,
the rope still attached to a bouquet
of dirty white seaweed, flowering
a heart of spilled brains.

I ran and ran.

But still these hearts came after me.

A washed sycamore leaf, hanging
from its stalk, another torn heart.
I smoothed away the debris of its journey,
and found a cobweb, fined and thinned,
the perfect outline of a pointed heart,
like the one I used to have.

I could risk this one,
I thought. So light, it's indestructible.
A North wind could blow right through
and break nothing. But I let go the stalk,
watched it fly along the wave foam.

And fished my own heart from its jaggedy
rock pool, because I remembered
my heart had never learned to swim.

# The Stomach Speaks

*Michael Malone*

I am the Principal Organ of Digestion.
The solution and reduction
of your food rests with me.
I have two mouths.

So feed me.

*I* am the shape of an irregular cone
curved in on itself, presenting a base
rounded like the heel of a silk purse.
Below the supposed-to-be-flexible
diaphragm and the poisonous, gossiping
liver, but above the odious colon. Naturally.

So feed me.

Examine me.
Ignore my mucus lining and you'll see
two polished extremities
two distinguished borders.
Oh, and did I mention, two mouths?

Feed me.

When gloriously full, distended,
tight with sugars and processed fat
I push away that dilatory heart
force up the great-I-am-Mr Diaphragm.
But when empty (as seems mostly to be the case)
I have to face your liver's left lobe
with its jaundiced thoughts,
keep my back to that sniping spleen,
and take the full weight
of your heavy, fur-lined heart.

Let me remind you of the noise I can make.
Think, ship's horn.
Think, elephant's trumpet.
Think social outcast.
Then feed me. Feed me well.

# Roasting Vegetables For Lunch

*Sheila Templeton*

We did the shopping first.
In Laiguelia market, the morning stretched
lazy arms. We stroked glossy purple aubergines,
held powdery-lilac swollen heads of garlic,
weighed single tomatoes. Each one
would have made a workman's lunch.

Then the slow walk home with string bags
criss crossing their raffia taut on creamy-brown
potatoes, like lace over a girl's slim thigh.
Back in the cool dark kitchen, we eased knots
of earth out of hidden places, sluicing skin
squeaky clean; trimmed and sliced, discarding
the unnecessary. Spread fresh butter,
green-golden olive oil, lapping, overlapping
layers, trusting the magic of alchemy;
which came, hot from the charcoal oven.

Well-polished metal blackened with promise.
Sweet potatoes soft peachy orange. Onion hearts
milky silver glistening sweating garlic cloves crisped
melting inside stem courgettes cut lengthwise
gleaming carrots saffron coloured juices
browned butter and good olive oil smelling
of hot sun. Turnips yellow-orange gritty. Squash
quartered among crusted potatoes dipped in flour.

We taste and taste, crunching blackened twigs
of thyme and peppery marjoram to punctuate
all the soft flesh and juices running,
the pinky orange glistening on our skin.

# Date and Walnut Loaf

*Rowena M Love*

A tried and tested treat
for the lovelorn:

Take fat you've been chewing
with the sugar daddy;
add a good egg, lots of zest
then flowers
(self-raising saves effort!)
and some old fruit.
Moisten with alcohol then mix well;
ideally there should be plenty of dough.

Bake at a high temperature –
dates should be hot, hot, hot.
Final texture should be soft and giving –
definitely not crusty.

Take care when serving:
taken prematurely, it'll be overly fresh;
wait too long and you'll find it's crumbly.

For maximum appreciation,
butter them up first
(middle-aged spread is an acquired taste).
Why not have jam on it too?

It could be a recipe for disaster
so use your loaf –
enjoy the dates
but avoid all nuts.

## Doing Lunch

*Jim Hughes*

We were there at the table
but not in our eyes.
We observed from a distance,
watching ourselves read from
dog-eared scripts.

There were excuses.
So many unshared years.
They marked the distance between us
across the white tablecloth.

We fingered fine wine glasses
and folded thin laughter over on itself
to plug the gaps.

We arm-wrestled for fame before forty.
The signals were coded but clear.
Skill with wine list and menu,
names dropped
with careless precision

Swilling dregs around coffee cups,
our conversation stiffened and stumbled
into credit cards and coats.

We're still straining for that
final handshake and each other's eyes.

# Bitter Sweet

*Sheila Templeton*

I'd love to write a poem outside,
while you read a book.
And I might show you a line
while you look. At me.
You could tell me what
you are reading. Or not.
I'd love to sit with you
for a very long time
under a tree by the ocean.
I'd search for the flattest stone,
skiff it across silver-topped waves
and laugh a lot.

We'd have a picnic and I'd listen,
(but only one more time)
while you tell me how your mother
made sandwiches destined to curl up
their corners on the kitchen table,
as she raged and murdered your picnic.
And how you don't trust women,
especially those who love to eat outside.

But I'd feed you the tiniest pieces,
so you could swallow the possibility
of love and commitment and all
those other scary words.

I'd love to drink too much wine
under dark vines, then retire
to the cool white sheets of afternoon.
I'd love to meet in town for coffee,
at three o'clock. But allow ourselves
to be diverted into the very back row
of the pictures and sit holding hands,
watching a film we don't understand.

# Note fur Postie

Michael Malone

Jeest wan, ye ken?
Ah wid huv liked jeest wan.

It wid huv been pink
of coorse. A subtle pink.
Jeest a suggestion o blush

n nane o yur roses
teddy bears n luv herts

n nane o yur daft wee
crude poems wae no even
a whispur o violets bein blue

...ken whit?

Bugger that.
It wid huv been SCARLET pink
pink as a brothel
pink as a bride the moarnin' eftur.

N the bears wid be skippin
n dancin. Bloody hunners o thum.
Richt acroass the sideboard
size o caird, carryin' wan rose
fur every day o the year
n waerin' a luv hert
the size o a fuckin' coo
oan thur chist.

N the poem wid be crap,
crap but funny. Full
o bums n wullies
n roses bein rid
n blue fuckin' violets.

It wid make me laff
so it wid. Until the tears
rolled doon ma cheeks.

# Postcard

*Michael Malone*

It floated onto his doormat
a week later. The scene a joy
of marble paving, fountain in mid-dance
and summer gilded rooftops.

Memory of sharp light
forced his eyes to narrow,
the hum of traffic
started its song in his ear.

The breeze from the veil of water
cooled the flesh of his neck
as he considered home,
a troubled wife and errant son.

Her smile nudged aside his thoughts.
He remembers glancing around,
sure such a smile was for another,
younger man. 'Three wishes
will ease your troubles.'

'I think my first already granted,' he replied.
While the rooftops were dusted silver,
they settled into an easy chat
like friends never parted.

Holding the card, feet planted
strong on his doorstep,
he smiles clear at his wife,
turns over the card and reads,
'Here you were wishing.'

# Love, Nil

*Rowena M Love*

Too short? Too tall? Or not at all
the type they seek? I feel a freak!
Too fat? Too thin? Wrong-coloured skin?
'Pick me! Pick me!' my heart-felt plea,
but still I sit the bench, unfit
for them to choose. Each time, I lose,
just watch, it seems till all are teams
of two, but me – a referee
in friends' affairs. As if I care
how well they've scored. Oh God! I'm bored
of sitting here. Don't want to hear
their play by play of yesterday:
how fancy feet defied defeat,
almost misses, winning kisses,
that perfect catch! The blessed match
can go to hell and love, as well –
I've had enough, don't give a stuff
… then heavy sigh just one more try –
'Pick me! Pick me! Oh please! Pick me!'

# Heaven

*Jim Hughes*

As I walked by the shoreline,
I thought about Heaven.

There will be squash courts, of course,
and a huge lecture theatre
full of attentive angels
who'll clatter their wings
in rapturous applause.

Often we'll sit somewhere high, you and I.
We'll hold hands and watch light paint ever-
changing patterns
on the sea, with a misty island on the horizon.

And we'll weep with joy.

Then I thought:
we have all that right now.
All except the angels that is,

But then ... I have you!

# You've Had Your Chips

*Sheila Templeton*

Ah' ll have chips please.
Ye know where ye are
wi' a bag o' chips.
And ye know exactly
what they'll cost.

They're always sizzlin' hot
on a Saturday night,
when you want them.
Nae need tae wait
fur the final whistle.

Chips don't get drunk
an' swear 'Ah love ye darlin.'
Niver promise tae phone
and then disappear
into mysterious silence.

Chips are reliable.
They sit there in yer hand.
You know you're in charge
wi' chips. Sure it's messy
if ye take them intae yer bed.
Whit's new?

No, nothin' oan the side,
thank you.

Just ma bag o' chips.

## Dream

*Jim Hughes*

You're the one that got away,
the dream that slipped the net.

'Got you,' I thought,
your scales gleaming
as you skated across the ceiling of your world.

But no such luck,
all I have
is the swirl on the surface
the flash of your tail.

# Slow Start

*Jim Hughes*

It's taking me a while
to get going this morning,
playing with fragments of images
to see which one sparkles.

In the end
they all glow a little
and promise more.

Smiling in their sleep,
they make dreamy noises,
which almost rhyme.

# Ma Valentine

*Michael Malone*

Ah remembur it like it wiz yisturday.
Kin it be twinty five year ago?
You wur fun oan the loo
they said.
Deid as a dodo
they said.
But, ah still sen' ye a caird.

Every Feb 14 ah sen' wan.
Wha's like ye, ah write
Damn few, n you're the wan who's deid.
'Cept ah don't bulieve it.
Ah reckin you're stashed awa
wae Marilyn n JFK, laughin'
et aw the dafties that fell fur it.

'Coz if you're deid, whit happens
tae ma dreams? Dae they hing oot
like yisturday's washin, waitin
for the weather tae chainge?
Diz the air squeez oot thum like
a long fart fae a whoppee cushin'
flattened by sum guy's fat erse.
Or ur they embalmed like a photay
in sumbuddy else's album?

Bit, don' wurry, sun
ah'll keep oan sendin' ye a caird
every Feb 14, till the coos moo hame,
till they nail ma coaffin shut,
till we meet up in Graceland.

# Ring of Brodgar

*Rowena M Love*

On that summer day,
it was easy
to hear echoes of Skara Brae's storm
in the whispering tide,
feel Viking fingers in Maeshowe's runes,
but the Ring…
the Ring stood like a palisade,
its crooked teeth biting at fierce blue sky,
gritting them at colours' sharpness
as it trapped me, obstinately, in the present.

Then, closing my eyes,
I touched a megalith.
It was cracked by more than four
millennia of frosts,
bearded with lichen,
but as a lark sang sagas
like bards of old
I could feel rough hands
on the June-warmed stone
reaching along time's ley line
to join with mine.

Just imagination? Perhaps.
Yet the same sun
shone on us both.

# Morning Stones

*Jim Hughes*

Two white stones
on the window ledge
absorb the morning light.

They reflect back
a hundred subtleties of tone,
and a billion years
of birthing galaxies.

# Now

*Sheila Templeton*

Stay silent.
Allow stillness
to settle in your heart.

Don't try to hog tie
the present to keep
control of the future.

It doesn't work
like that.

You only strangle
the beauty
of the moment.

The sweetest music
is the sound of now.

Allow it. Listen to it.

That way, the future
can spill out
in all its perfection,
from the fullness
of the present.

# Owed to My Accountant

*Rowena M Love*

*for Sheila*

I was a numerical novice
in search of enlightenment;
seeking elaboration
of the taxman's strict code.

In a flash,
my financial guru
had me flexing my figures
in the Lotus 1-2-3 position;
grim accounts of this pilgrim
soon in holy order,
any surplus donning the surplice
of allowable expenses.

Yea, I do believe
her Sage counselling brought balance.
My prayers all answered:
no trip down the Suwannee
thanks to my swami
of sums.

# City Summer

*Jim Hughes*

Traffic bollards cast grubby shadows
on hot Mayfair pavements. Builder's dust
blurs the edges.

Workmen, short on shovels, lean on discontent,
sun red bellies hang over elasticated shorts.
Sweat runs from under their blue hard hats.

City gents, defying heat, stick to grey pinstripe,
which, in turn, sticks to them.

Whiz kids boast red braces
over sweat stained stripey shirts.
Their faces ooze lunch time wine.

Red traffic lights force grey fumes
from shuddering exhausts.

Tourists from Tokyo, pollution connoisseurs,
sniff smog delicately, and mark it out of ten.

# New Minted Morning

*Rowena M Love*

There's a hush
then frantic trading
as thrush, blackbird, chaffinch
tender loudly for their share
of the growing light,
jostling the air
with bids and counter bids.

Mr Wind, invisible investor,
riffles bankrolls from the trees
while Dawn idly tosses
her golden coin.

Shepherds are silent partners,
profiting from Spring's
capital investment.
Their advice:
bright futures depend on today
ending in the red.

## Grace

*Jim Hughes*

If God was there in that cold little church,
hovering over your baptism,
he must have allowed himself a wry smile.

Grace, you were christened,
and grace you would pursue, forlornly,
for the rest of your flint hard life.

You would have settled for forgiveness,
but that was just as scarce,
as your crow black voices
would relentlessly remind you
year after year.

Until you finally said

Amen.

# Drinking Jesus' Blood

*Michael Malone*

Sister Mary tears me from my dream,
mouth pursed white like the lip of a drawstring bag.
Again, urine had seeped from my Judas bladder.
Pyjamas in deep, wet, cotton folds burn from belly to knee.

Sister Mary, a window-less room and a bath of ice water.
The drum in my ear shivers
at the machine gun rattle of my teeth.
Naked, I hide my hairless sex behind bone-thin hands.
'Get your hands away, you dirty little pervert.'
My mouth opens, my hands move from sin, then back.

Cold water bites flesh.
Skin and muscle shrink to a tight sheath.
Her black sleeves rolled up,
forearms white as a frosted soul.
She tries to find suds in iced carbolic.
I bite on the questions:
will my teeth chip or break from clattering,
how much will the tooth fairy give if they are in crumbs?
Rubbed with stiff towel till skin heats, blue to pink.

In the Sacristy with Jim Docherty, the other Altar Boy,
itch of shame replaces the nip of urine.
'Wet The Bed,' he chants.
'Shut it, Big Nose,' I bruise his arm – and don white.
'Lads,' says Father Kieran, tousles our brylcreemed heads
and leaves us with a chalice full of communion wine.

The vessel grows until it shrinks the room,
I lean forward to touch it.
Jim's eyebrows bounce off his hairline, 'Bet you wouldn't.'
I grip the stem in answer to his hushed taunt.
Heart charging at my ribcage I moisten lips, and pour.
Teeth and tongue fur sour before I force open my throat.
A blazing bolus flares a trail to my stomach.

Jim, slack mouthed with fear and awe,
'Oh-oh, that's a sin. You've just drank Jesus' blood.'
'Aye, and it tastes like piss!'

# Snawy Beach

*Rowena M Love*

Brockit[1] as collie dugs wi snaw an brook,
Troon shore plays fesh[2] wi folk.
Kelpies[3] ramp in puppy games,
tossin thirsel lik sticks
throu a ruff o waves,
kist[4] an kyte
white as wrack wid[5].
Snawy hackles liftet bi last nicht's frost,
weans tug the fur tae snawba's,
or smuith it wi thir sled,
penny dugged[6] bi parents
aye in ahint[7].

[1] *brockit* = black and white;
  *brook* = a deep layer of seaweed cast ashore by
  stormy weather.
[2] *fesh* = fetch
[3] *kelpies* = a mischievous young person; a water demon;
  *ramp* = romp boisterously.
[4] *kist* = chest; *kyte* = stomach
[5] *wrack wid* = driftwood
[6] *penny dug* = a dog that follows its master very closely
[7] *in ahint* = walking to heel

# Hairst Meen

*Sheila Templeton*

Sleekit stoats, we slippet ower i dyke
through coorse thistles, reeshlin stalks.
Boo't twa-faal[1] lik half shut knives, mowdied[2]
a labyrinth far nae minotaur cud roar,
nae hostages be sacrificed fur ony king.
A warld o whisperin paths, swirlin
in still green corn, far we jinket[3] and ran,
caa'd wirsels deen[4], sprauchlin lik pups
in beaten halla chaumers. Breathin
in each ithers hert hemmer, fyle
i hairst meen's wyme[5] swalled gowd
through lang licht nichts. Ontil
i corn wis ready fir cuttin and bindin
and biggin intil glitterin stooks. Ontil
i clatterin combine chased aabody
oot, doon ti i hinmaist squaar heezen[6]
wi little herts, lugs pented flat,
ready ti rin fir life itsel. Ontil
i stooks stood sillered, leeful-leen[7],
ooner i licht i sich a different meen.

[1] *Boo't twa-faal* = bent double
[2] *moudied* = tunnelled like a mole
[3] *jinket* = played; chased each other; zigzagged
[4] *caa'd wirsels deen* = wore ourselves out
[5] *hairst meen's wyme* = harvest moon's womb
[6] *hinmaist squaar* = final square;
  *heezen* = swarming
[7] *leefull-leen* = solitary

## Weekend Cyclist

*Rowena M Love*

Sitting proud on the prow
of a saddle,
he sits stiff as a clipper's figurehead,
jacket luffing in the breeze.
Brine collects on his brow
like sea spray,
while the sound of breakers
rolls and crashes
through the trees he passes,
thanks to a freshening wind.

Knees piston,
until wheels whirl
like Waverley paddles
but his breath coughs,
more puffer than liner,
steam of exertion
funnelling in his wake.
Exhaustion's tide rises,
so he heads for home port
where his bike will be beached
for another week.

# Entomology: Genus Serious Cyclist

*Rowena M Love*

Pinned to the saddle,
a serious cyclist.
Handlebar antennae protrude
beneath glossy chitin helmet
that starts the curve
of his scarab shape.
Coloration varies:
light-swallowing black;
shimmering iridescence
of Day-Glo® kit;
or the intricate markings of sponsorship.
Like a water louse scurrying
across pond's surface,
he skims the road,
heart humming,
as his legs blur
to holograph visions of speed.

# Runnin' Fur A Marathon

*Michael Malone*

Ah membur runnin tae buy a Marathon,
poakit money too hoat fur cloath
swimmin in sweat in ma palm.
Whit if the coin meltit in value?
Thur wid be nae toaffee,
nae nougit, nae nuts and nae choac'lit, then.

Ah membur the slap o' saunshoe oan the road,
Mr Fraser's new cor wae the baw-shaped dent
croassin the road afore ah passed his hoose,
his roar, 'Ya wee shite, ah'll tell yur ol' man
and Faither McCluskie!'

Feelin brave, ah shoutit
'Shut it, ya ol baw-bag!'
wance ah goat roon the coarnur.

Heat oan the back o' ma legs.
Three Hail Mary's
and wan Oor Faither.

Ah membur reachin the path tae the shoap.
Hoo much enurgy ah hud. Ah could huv entured
The Run Everywhaur Event et the Olympics.

Ah membur the dug.
Ah membur the bark
Ah membur the teeth.

Ah jumpt high-pitched in the air
coin flashed doon the drain
ma Marathon burrit in sludge' n sin.

Ah membur runnin tae buy a Marathon.
Didnae get wan.

# Poetic Licence

*Rowena M Love*

Where do I apply for my poetic licence?
The post office? P.O.?

Oh, where do I go?
Stanza poet – he'll know!

Where's the slot for the metre?
So as to create that world-beater.

Is there a secret code in scanning?
Putting the poet behind bars.

Where do I walk the doggerel –
Or does it run?

Iambic or biro, which pen is mightier?
Plain verse, rhyme, or something flightier?

How can free verse cost so much?
Have I lost touch?

I just want to be a poet.
To try it...

But I find my way
Bard – no entry!

# The Dug 'N Bone

*Michael Malone*

See that phone? Ay ringin'
Ay ringin' its wee heid aff
Ay ringin like it wis desperate
fur sumbuddy, onybuddy, tae answer.
'N the thing is – we dae. We react
juist like Pavlov's Dugs. 'Cept
they goat sumthin' tae eat
fur thur trouble. Whit dae we get?
Sum wassock wantin' tae sell
sum shite we've already goat.
Ah say, naw, don't answer it.
Let it ring till it explodes.
Let it ring till they gie up.
Let it ring till the Pope stoaps
wearing his funny hat.

But then, sumtimes it's silent
fur days, weeks even. Silent
as an empty nest. Ah wiz
in the bath, the ither nicht.
Relaxin, 'Chillin oot'
when it stertit its mental ring.
Ah wiz oot the bath, doon the stairs
soakin' the carpet, in the skuddy
hopin' nane o ma neeghbours
wid see me thru the windae.
'Hullo', Ah said, fightin'
tae keep the hope oot ma voice.

'Can I speak to Rodney, please?'
'Rodney?' Dae ah sound like
a bloody Rodney, ah asked masel.
'Yuv the wrang nummer, hen,' Ah said.
'Oh dear, I am sorry,' she said. Sounded lovely,
sounded aboot the age o ma dochter,
sounded like she hud blonde hair;
big, broon eyes and a smile
warm enuff tae melt the polar ice cap.
'I hope I haven't disturbed you.'
'S'aw right, hen,' Ah said,
regrettin' ma tempur.
'The phone wiz ringin' oanyway.'

# Like a Visitor

*Sheila Templeton*

Your room's tidy.
You've left it
downie smoothed,
pillow sitting up
like a plump visitor.

I'm glad of this damp towel
crumpling a corner.

'Okay to have a bath,' you said.

Okay was you
sprawling careless limbs,
sloth draped
over the settee.
A cornflake mountain
drowned in milk.
Locust stripped fridge,
Dead Head Comics,
flicking T.V. channels,
driving me daft.
Not hearing
until I squatted down
into your eyeballs.

'What's that you're sayin' Mum?'

I'm saying,

That time you slammed
a fist into thin wall,
and you... wet newspaper,
chalky plaster mixed
in a jam jar,
tongue sticking out
in concentration,
covering the hole,

'Calm down Mother. It's FINE!'

Has left a space,
an empty place.
My hand finds it,
every time I climb
these stairs.

A bumpy, gritty patch,
unpainted and never
sanded smooth.

# Letting Go

*Michael Malone*

The sculptor runs her thumb
along the line of blade
as sharp as desire,
feeding the metal's wish
with her iron. She prays

to the mirror that her past
will not determine the length
depth and curl of her strokes,
will not breathe sentience
into a twin of her. She pauses

at the first cut, feels the first
contraction and accepts her purpose.
Working hard now, breathing laboured,
sweat pearls on her forehead
weeps into her hair. She carves

a smooth brow, eyes wide, pupils large
chin strong, shoulders square,
breasts firm but yielding and prays
the heart beneath works
trim and true. She pushes

down to the plain of the stomach
flows to the flare of hips
falters at her daughter's sex.
Knowledge is imparted before
flesh is cleaved to a sensuous swell.
Limbs are strengthened by feet
that know their direction. Carving
the navel remains till last. She fears
cutting the umbilicus needs an edge
sharper than any she owns.

# Calyx

*Sheila Templeton*

You sexy little thing.
Georgia noticed you, half hidden,
coy in the back row of the wedding bouquet and slid
you out from the other stems. She carried you home,
all the way to her studio, to see to you. Stroke your
silky hood, drift fingertips down that snowy calyx
to your stamen tip, gorgeous in farm buttery yellow,
dusted in pollen and ready for anything.

You lucky thing.
All these nerve endings under the skin,
enough of each gender
to have your own bed bonanza.
No need to comb the New Mexico desert
looking for a mate.

You have it all.
Woman's parts petalled soft, swaddled,
parting for your little bit of man, en suite, complete.
No wonder you were perfectly happy,
standing perjink, prim,
listening to the first bars of the wedding march.

But Georgia spotted you. And here you are, sitting
in her favourite vase looking out at Taos mountain,
as she paints you into her life.
Lingering over each line,
bringing known from unknown. Paying attention.
And, not content with that, set you up on curvy,
split tailed dolphins cavorting under your root.
In case we'd somehow failed to get the message.

# Greek Statues

*Michael Malone*

Wiz et the museum the ither day.
Fur a wee spoat a culture.
Luked et some smashin pictures
then ah saw a sign fur the statues.
Mebbe's a chance tae see
a bare breest:
a chance tae ogle
wi'oot gettin called a pervert.
But, DISAPPOINTED,
they were maistly o' men.
Ah mean, ye don't really want to luk there
dae ye, s'a bit sick intit, lukin
et other men's tadgers? N', thur no
the brawest things in the wurld,
ah reckin God wiz hivin a laugh
when he came up wi them.
Ah luked et a few, afore a realized,
sumbuddy had lobbed aff wan soadger's tadger.
He hud the spear, the war helmet
a rerr perr a baws, but a raggedy space
whaur his tadger should've been.

Then ah luked et some mair.
Richt enuff, no a knob in sicht.
Weel, except fur wan wee boay.
Couldnae really ca' that a wullie.
So who did it? Who wiz the
Tadger-Lobber-Affer? The De-Knobber?
The art wurld's Mrs Bobbit?
Mebbe it wiz wan a they Victorians?
They couldnae even staun the sicht
o' a bare table leg. A row a wullies
wid've been enuff tae gie them the vapours
fur a month a Mondays. Mebbe it wiz wan
o they Suffragettes. Ah kin juist see her
'Eftur brekfast, n' afore ah chain masel
tae they railin's, ah think I'll juist go
n' choap aff a few wullies.'

Ah hud a close luk et wan,
in the interests of science, ye unnerstan'…
n' the wound was still raw.

# Giverny

*Rowena M Love*                    *'Hormis la peinture et le jardinage, je ne suis bon à rien[1].'*

A mirrored bridge
echoes painter reflected in gardener,
arabesque so exact
that up could be down, down up,
air, colour, light more real
than mere planks of wood.

Irises the deep purple of pleasure
unfurl at the edge,
tinting the day with midnight.
Painting them stained his fingers
just as earth daubed his hands
from their planting.

He serves us blossom on water lily trays.
They blush at the coquetry
whispered by wind through willows
whose pashmina folds swirl
in an exuberance of green,
tasselled edges teasing water
where pine shimmers to lime:
shadows in a pool
playing kiss and tell
with nymphs
as the bowed lips of the bridge
and its reflection
gasp at a dragonfly's iridescence.

[1] *I'm good for nothing except painting and gardening'*
Claude Monet

# Poem for Kay

*Sheila Templeton*

Small rainbows filled your sitting room
spilling from the crystal in the window.
Even the dog had a jewelled stencil
winking on a pale barley flank,
like a sailor dancing his tattooed lady.

Always music. Remember Van the Man
and those rolling hills? And raspberry pavlova,
no spoons allowed for whipped cream
on chewy meringue and dripping, staining
grainy berries. Fingers only.
Your house was tasty.

You taught me the freedom of splashing
three bunches of singing yellow daffodils
in one white jug. Jumble sale mirrors
reflected your giant vision of ponds and paths,
hidden under rubble and waist-high grass.
And you, fag in hand, dwarfed by the spade,
pushing dark hair out of even darker eyes,
painting in the air how it was all to be.

A different canvas from those stacked about
your living space and on the walls. All you.
Shouting in colour. Or telling stories
of that monster black bear you wrestled
and sometimes won. But not at the end.

I can never imagine you at peace.
You'll be sitting in God's favourite restaurant,
writing a critique on a paper napkin,
to send to the chef in His kitchen, because
you will not say it's okay if it's not.

And how could you come back there
to eat, if you weren't honest? You'll be laughing
as you tip the waiter, because it's not his fault, is it?
And shouting again, probably in Anglo Saxon,
making your wonderful noise.
Stirring up the angels.

# The Missing Piece

*Michael Malone*

When you are dead…
when your voice no longer
chimes along the telephone wire,
when your energy dissipates
then reforms to feed memory,

I will bear your coffin
and rejoice in its weight;
itch to return to the murmur
of your papers, to that corner
shelf with book spines
delightedly gilded with titles
designed to offend a society
already decidedly impolite.

I will revisit that garden
in my mind forever yours,
weed out my preconceptions
plant some flowers of a darker hue
and relish the symmetry
of a jigsaw complete.

# Nothing

*Jim Hughes*

I shrink inwards,
wrap around myself
the thin warmth of fading sleep.

Cold wakefulness promises nothing
but a different nothing.

# After I Die

*Sheila Templeton*

*(after Jo Shapcott)*

I'm coming back on All Saints' Day

for your damson jam with the stones left in.
To sit in your lap. This time I'll wear

my satin bodice, leave the top hooks unfastened
spill creamy flesh on to your chest,
see you undone.

You might lose me in the crowds that day. Watch
by my grave. Scatter a trail of juicy poems

back to your flat. Perfume the air with music
for dirty dancing. Leave the door open

a little, so I can see all the candles you've lit.

# Treshnish Isles

*Jim Hughes*

They cluster like great sea creatures
conferring before a vast odyssey.

Waves froth from their tails
as they test their engines
and check ancient charts,
before casting loose.

One day… perhaps one day.

# Sligachan Sunset

*Rowena M Love*

Black Cuillin, climber magnet,
has rocks hedgehogging the ridge
with metal filings.
Evening dips sky's litmus red,
its acid etching shadows among the crags.

Far below, the Sligachan bubbles
like a science experiment gone mad
or fills Petri dish pools
with pink gel of sunset-tinted water
that quivers in the breeze.

Chemistry is perfect:
beyond where cottongrass swabs the banks,
a cuckoo calls, voice clear
in distilled peace of dusk.

## Comma

*Jim Hughes*

Did you notice me?

In that beautiful line,
that heart stopping phrase?

Did you notice me?
I bet you didn't.

Just a comma, the lowest ranking foot soldier
in punctuation's pecking order.

Smaller than a colon, the dictionary defines me.
A colon: two specks of fly shit on the page
of history.

But me, this tail of mine relates me to my
glamorous cousin.
That flaming longhaired star, the comet.

So when next you hold your breath,
in that blissful hiatus that heightens desire,
think of me.

That pause
comma
between this heartbeat
comma
and the next.

# Clutter

*Jim Hughes*

The clutter creeps back.

Each paper invites another
to join its lazy sprawl

Every one an unmade decision
wrapped in a good intention.

Or perhaps an amoeba,
the protozoa of a poem.

# Acknowledgements

The poets wish to acknowledge the following places where some of this work has previously appeared, or been broadcast:

The Art of Bicycling *Breakaway Books ;*
The Coffee House; Cutting Teeth;
The Clydesiders Trilogy *Margaret Thomson Davis*
Eclipse; End of the Millennium;
The Fireside Book *D C Thompson;*
Friends and Enemies *Wild Goose Publications*
Hay and Stardust *Wild Goose Publications*
Helicon Poetry Magazine; The Herald; iota;
The Interpreter's House; Ju Ju; Markings;
McCash Poetry Competition Anthology;
New Writing Scotland *Volumes 16, 17, 21 and 23;*
Orbis; Poetry Monthly; Poetry Scotland;
Poetry Nottingham International;
Praying for the Dawn *Wild Goose Publications*
PsychoPoetica; Quantum Leap; Radio Clyde;
Radio Scotland; Reach Poetry Magazine;
The Scots Magazine; Scottish Islands Explorer;
The Wallace Muse *Luath Press;*
World Wide Writers International;
Yesterday's Patna And The Lost
Villages Of Doon Valley *Donald Reid*

Some of the poems in this collection were finalists in the following competitions:
Scottish International Open Poetry Competition
The McCash Prize for Scots Poetry
The Dorothy Dunbar Trophy

# Jim Hughes

Born in Ayrshire, Jim followed the West of Scotland tradition of engineering which led him into a successful career as a manager, industrialist, and University professor. The main theme of his many tasks and challenges in this work has been the behaviour, conflict and growth of individuals in the complex and frustrating context of work. In his attempt to make sense of, and contribute something new to the many paradoxes he encountered, he sought, and continues to seek clues in the fields of psychology and spirituality. His writing, both prose and poetry, attempts to share some of these insights.

*Poems in this collection:*
A Touching Place; Angry Prayer; Burnout; Christmas Child; City Summer; Clutter; Comma; Doing Lunch; Dream; Genocide; Grace; Heaven; Heron; Morning Stones; Nothing; Old Hat; Osiris; Playground; Scream; Silence; Slow Start; Treshnish Isles

# Rowena M Love

Rowena is based in Troon, in the West of Scotland. She started writing seriously in 1997 and since then has racked up many successes. She has had hundreds of poems published in a wide variety of places and has done well in competitions, too. She also writes non-fiction, with many articles to her credit. You can find out more about Rowena, and see further samples of her work on her website: www.rowenamlove.co.uk.
Rowena is Writer in Residence for Ayrshire charity Writability and is on the Live Literature Scotland database operated by the Scottish Book Trust. She is happy to give workshops on writing, give talks and readings of her work.

*Poems in this collection:*
A Proverb Moon; Date and Walnut Loaf;
Entomology: Genus Serious Cyclist;
Feeding the Birds; For Annie; Giverny; Hot Tub;
Keekin In; Lost Villages o' Doon; Love, Nil;
Makin Pancakes; New Minted Morning;
Owed to My Accountant; Poetic Licence;
Presents and Absence; Ring of Brodgar;
Sligachan Sunset; Snawy Beach;
Song of Wallace; The Carousel; The Causeway;
The Dolphin; Weekend Cyclist

# Michael Malone

Michael, from Ayr, has worked as a Financial Adviser, Bookseller, Life Coach, Creative Writing Lecturer and Poet. Since he began writing he has been widely published in literary magazines and anthologies. His greatest pleasure has been working with the other Makar Press Poets as they spread the word on poetry the length and breadth of the country. "People really enjoy our particular blend of the personal, the profound and the piquant," he said. We are sure if he could have thought of another word beginning with 'P' he would have stuck that in as well. He wants his epitaph to read – 'I never ate enough Mars bars.'

*Poems in this collection:*
A Daughter's Diary; A Welcome Touch; Drinking Jesus' Blood; Dug an Bone; Father Martin; For Worse; Greek Statues; Guiding Hand; H M Iolaire; In the Raw; Letting Go; Like a Sneeze; Lucozade, Grapes and Silence; Ma Valentine; Note fur Postie; Postcard; Runnin fur a Marathon; Sunday Morning; The Clearances; The Missing Piece; The Stomach Speaks; Thoroughly Modern Man; Veni, Vidi, Vici

# Sheila Templeton

Sheila Templeton was born in Aberdeen, then spent an itinerant childhood ranging from Rannoch Moor to Dar-es-Salaam and back to Aberdeenshire. Though she left her roots forty years ago, her work still draws on that rich Buchan landscape. She now lives right by the sea in Ayrshire which 'still feels like dancing at a surprise party'.

The beach dancing led to a first poetry collection Slow Road Home, as well as publication in many magazines, anthologies and readings on Radio Scotland. She has also been successful in several national poetry competitions. In addition to poetry, Sheila writes fiction for adults and children. She is currently trying to learn the Argentine Tango.

*Poems in this collection:*
A Bonnie Fechter; After I Die; Bitter Sweet; Breast Screening; Calyx; Communion; Daddy's Girl; Going Home; Hairst Meen; Hot Chick; Like A Visitor; Little Sleeve; Love Underground; Miss Sixty; Now; Poem for Kay; Requiem for a Son; Roasting Vegetables for Lunch; Scars; Sitting with Maisie; Summertime; Taking New Heart; You've Had Your Chips